That's Not a Pet!

CAN I HAVE A PET EAGLE?

By Michou Franco

Gareth Stevens Publishing

Please visit our website, www.garethstevens.com. For a free color catalog of all our high-quality books, call toll free 1-800-542-2595 or fax 1-877-542-2596.

Library of Congress Cataloging-in-Publication Data

Names: Franco, Michou, author.
Title: Can I have a pet eagle? / Michou Franco.
Description: New York : Gareth Stevens Publishing, [2019] | Series: That's not a pet! | Includes index.
Identifiers: LCCN 2017040514| ISBN 9781538217849 (library bound) | ISBN 9781538217863 (pbk.) | ISBN 9781538217870 (6 pack)
Subjects: LCSH: Bald eagle–Juvenile literature.
Classification: LCC QL696.F32 F74 2019 | DDC 598.9/43–dc23
LC record available at https://lccn.loc.gov/2017040514

First Edition

Published in 2019 by
Gareth Stevens Publishing
111 East 14th Street, Suite 349
New York, NY 10003

Editor: Therese Shea
Designer: Sarah Liddell

Photo credits: Cover, p. 1 FloridaStock/Shutterstock.com; p. 5 Milan Zygmunt/Shutterstock.com; p. 7 Raimon Santacatalina/Shutterstock.com; pp. 9, 24 (beak) ChiccoDodiFC/Shutterstock.com; pp. 11, 24 (talon) Teri Virbickis/Shutterstock.com; p. 13 Karel Bartik/Shutterstock.com; p. 15 Brenda Smith DVM/Shutterstock.com; p. 17 Chris Humphries/Shutterstock.com; p. 19 Kovalenko/Shutterstock.com; p. 21 Paul Reeves Photography/ Shutterstock.com; p. 23 mikluha_maklai/Shutterstock.com.

Printed in the United States of America

CPSIA compliance information: Batch #CS18GS: For further information contact Gareth Stevens, New York, New York at 1-800-542-2595.

Contents

I want a pet.
I want an eagle!

Eagles are large birds.
There are many kinds.

All have a sharp beak.

They have claws
called talons.

Eagles are birds of prey.
That means they hunt!

They can fly for hours.
They hunt animals below.

The bald eagle is
one kind of eagle.
It isn't bald.
It has a white head.

It eats fish!

Eagles need to fly.
They need to hunt.
They need to live in nests.

Eagles aren't good pets.
I'll see them at the zoo!

Words to Know

beak

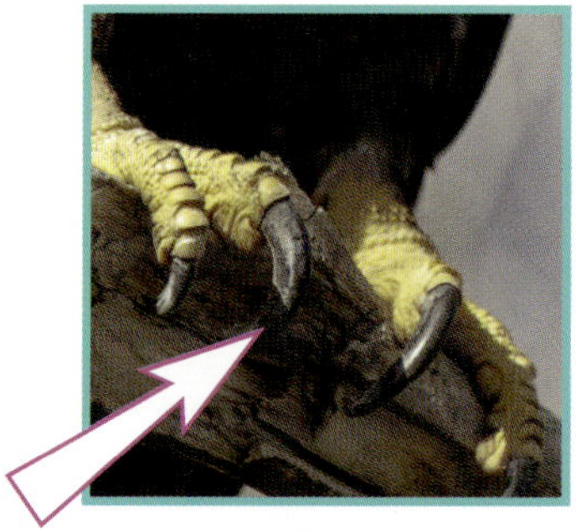

talon

Index